NAVIGATING THE SPECTRUM

A Parent's Guide to Understanding Autism

Tony Shark

Shark Brain Industries

CONTENTS

FOREWORD

As you open this book, you embark on a profoundly meaningful journey, one that will deepen your understanding of autism and, more importantly, your connection with a truly remarkable individual: your child. Autism is not a barrier to be overcome; it is a unique way of being, a distinct lens through which the world is seen, felt, and experienced. Within this spectrum lies an extraordinary richness of thought, creativity, and perspective, and your child holds a part of that brilliance.

Parenting is always an adventure, filled with love, challenges, and growth. But when your journey involves autism, it becomes something even more transformative. You are given the opportunity to explore a world where conventional rules and expectations often do not apply. Instead, you learn to celebrate the incredible diversity of human experience and the boundless potential of the human spirit.

"Navigating the Spectrum: A Parent's Guide to Understanding Autism" is more than just a guide; it is a companion, offering both practical insights and heartfelt encouragement. This book acknowledges the wide range of emotions you may feel, from uncertainty and fear to awe and joy. It speaks to the immense love and dedication you bring to your parenting and affirms that these are the most important tools you have as you guide your child through a world that might not always understand them.

Autistic children possess extraordinary qualities. They may see patterns where others see chaos, hear melodies in the hum of everyday life, or express their thoughts in ways that challenge and expand our understanding of communication. They teach us patience, empathy, and the beauty of seeing the world through fresh eyes. Their presence is a gift, not only to their families but to the wider world.

This book is written with the belief that knowledge empowers. It provides you with the tools to navigate your child's unique journey, helping you advocate for their needs, celebrate their strengths, and foster their growth. It is also a reminder that you are not alone. Countless families walk a similar path, and there is a community of love, wisdom, and shared experience waiting to support you.

As you read, take comfort in knowing that there is no "perfect" way to parent an autistic child. There is only your way, path defined by love, guided by understanding, and enriched by the moments of connection and discovery you share with your child. Remember to celebrate the victories, no matter how small they may seem, and to be gentle with yourself on the harder days.

Your child's journey is one of beauty, wonder, and immense potential. They are not just navigating the spectrum; they are navigating life with courage and authenticity. And with your unwavering love and support, they can shine in their own incredible way.

It is my hope that this book inspires you, empowers you, and reminds you of the profound privilege it is to nurture and learn from your unique and extraordinary child.

CHAPTER 1: UNDERSTANDING AUTISM AND ITS SPECTRUM

The Spectrum Explained

The concept of the autism spectrum is a profound and multifaceted notion that reshapes how we perceive and understand individuals with autism. It serves as a reminder that autism is not a singular condition but rather a diverse range of experiences and characteristics. Each child on the spectrum presents a unique blend of strengths and challenges, influenced by their environment, personality, and support systems. Embracing this spectrum encourages parents and guardians to appreciate the individuality of their children, fostering an atmosphere of acceptance and love that is critical for their development.

Understanding the early signs of autism is essential for timely intervention and support. Symptoms can manifest differently across the spectrum, with some children displaying noticeable signs as early as 18 months, while others may be identified later. Common indicators include difficulties with communication, challenges in social interactions, and atypical behaviors or interests. By educating themselves on these early signs, parents can become vigilant observers of their child's development, ensuring that they seek professional help when necessary. Early diagnosis paves the way for personalized educational strategies and therapeutic approaches that can significantly enhance a child's growth.

Education plays a crucial role in the lives of children on the autism spectrum. Tailoring educational strategies to meet individual needs can help unlock their potential and foster a love of learning. Techniques such as visual supports, structured environments, and social skills training can create a rich learning experience. Collaborating closely with teachers and educational professionals allows parents to advocate for their child's needs effectively. With the right educational support, children can thrive academically and socially, gaining essential skills that will serve them throughout their lives.

Sensory processing is another critical aspect of autism that affects daily experiences. Many children on the spectrum might be hyper-sensitive or hypo-sensitive to sensory input, which can lead to challenges in various environments. Understanding sensory processing allows parents to create supportive home and school environments that cater to their child's sensory needs. Simple adjustments, such as providing a quiet space for relaxation or incorporating calming sensory activities, can make a significant difference in a child's ability to navigate the world around them. With this awareness, parents can help their children build resilience and develop coping strategies.

Finally, as children grow, the journey continues into adolescence and adulthood, where the focus shifts toward employment and independence. Advocacy and awareness are vital components in supporting individuals on the autism spectrum as they transition into the workforce. Encouraging the development of social skills, vocational training, and self-advocacy empowers individuals to pursue their passions and contribute meaningfully to society. By fostering an inclusive environment and promoting understanding, we can help dismantle barriers, paving the way for a future where individuals on the spectrum can thrive and inspire those around them.

Myths And Misconceptions

Myths and misconceptions surrounding autism can create barriers to understanding and acceptance. One prevalent myth is that autism is solely a childhood disorder, leading to the belief that individuals outgrow it. In reality, autism is a lifelong condition that may evolve in how it manifests as a person ages. Understanding that autism does not simply disappear can help parents and guardians recognize the continuous need for support and resources throughout their child's life. This truth empowers families to seek appropriate educational strategies and therapeutic approaches tailored to their loved ones' evolving needs.

Another common misconception is that all individuals on the autism spectrum lack empathy or emotional connection. This stereotype oversimplifies the rich emotional world of autistic individuals. Many possess deep feelings and form meaningful relationships, though they may express their emotions differently. By fostering a better understanding of these diverse emotional expressions, parents and guardians can advocate for their children, ensuring that their unique ways of connecting are recognized and valued in society. This shift in perspective can encourage more inclusive environments that nurture social skills development.

The idea that autism is caused by bad parenting persists, despite overwhelming evidence to the contrary. This harmful myth can lead to feelings of guilt and inadequacy among parents, detracting from their ability to focus on their child's strengths and needs. It is essential to acknowledge that autism is a neurodevelopmental condition with complex genetic and environmental factors. By dispelling this misconception, parents can embrace their role as advocates for their children, seeking out support networks that promote understanding and acceptance rather than blame.

Another prevalent myth is that individuals with autism are unable to lead successful, fulfilling lives. This misconception often stems from a limited view of what success entails. In reality, many individuals on the spectrum thrive in various fields, including technology, art, and business. By highlighting stories of success and resilience, we can inspire parents and guardians to nurture their child's passions and strengths, fostering a belief in their potential. Encouraging a view of success that is personal and unique to each individual can open doors to employment and career development opportunities.

Lastly, the notion that autism is a solitary journey is a

CHAPTER 2: EARLY SIGNS AND DIAGNOSIS OF AUTISM

Recognizing Early Signs

Recognizing the early signs of autism is a crucial step in ensuring that children receive the support they need to thrive. As parents and guardians, being aware of these signs can empower you to seek appropriate evaluations and interventions that can make a significant difference in your child's development. Early recognition is not just about identifying challenges; it is about understanding the unique ways in which your child perceives and interacts with the world. By tuning into these early indicators, you can create a nurturing environment that fosters growth, learning, and understanding.

One of the earliest signs to look for is the way your child engages with others. Many children on the spectrum may show limited eye contact or may not respond to their name being called. They might prefer to play alone rather than engage in interactive play with peers. These behaviors can be subtle but are important clues. Encouraging social interaction through playdates or group activities can help you observe how your child interacts with their peers, and it can also provide valuable opportunities for social skills development.

Another area to consider is communication. Children on the autism spectrum may exhibit delays in speech and language skills, or they may communicate in ways that are different from their peers, such as through gestures or pointing instead of using words. You might notice that your child has a unique way of expressing their needs and emotions, and it's essential to recognize and validate these forms of communication. Engaging in activities that promote language development, such as reading together or using visuals, can support your child's communication skills and enhance their ability to connect with others.

Sensory processing is another critical aspect to observe. Many children with autism may exhibit heightened sensitivity to sensory stimuli or may seek out sensory experiences in unusual ways. This could manifest as a strong reaction to loud noises, bright lights, or certain textures. By paying attention to your child's responses to their sensory environment, you can help create a comforting atmosphere that minimizes discomfort and maximizes their ability to explore and learn. Incorporating sensory-friendly activities into their daily routine can also promote self-regulation and emotional well-being.

Lastly, it's vital to approach the recognition of these signs with an open heart and mind. Early intervention can lead to substantial improvements in various areas of development, but it's essential to remember that every child is unique. Embracing your child's differences while advocating for their needs can empower both you and your child. Connecting with support networks, resources, and educational strategies tailored for children on the spectrum can provide invaluable guidance as you navigate this journey together. Each step you take to recognize and understand early signs is a step toward unlocking your child's potential and celebrating their individuality.

The Diagnostic Process

The diagnostic process for autism spectrum disorder (ASD) can feel overwhelming for parents and guardians, yet understanding its intricacies is essential in navigating this journey with confidence and hope. It begins with a series of assessments that evaluate a child's behavior, communication skills, and social interactions. Early signs may manifest in various ways, such as delayed speech, difficulties in making eye contact, or an unusual response to sensory stimuli. Recognizing these signs and seeking evaluation is a vital first step in addressing the unique needs of a child on the spectrum. Parents should remember that early intervention can lead to significantly improved outcomes, allowing children to thrive in their development.

Once parents decide to pursue a diagnosis, they typically engage with a multidisciplinary team composed of pediatricians, psychologists, and speech-language pathologists. These professionals use a combination of standardized tests and observational assessments to gather comprehensive information about the child's behavior in different environments. This collaborative approach ensures that all aspects of the child's development are considered, giving parents a clearer picture of their child's strengths and challenges. It is important for parents to actively participate in this process, as their insights and observations are invaluable.

Receiving a diagnosis can be an emotional experience, filled with a mix of relief and uncertainty. Many parents find solace in knowing that they are not alone in this journey, as support networks and resources are available. Understanding that a diagnosis does not define a child's potential can be liberating. Instead, it opens doors to tailored educational strategies, therapies, and interventions that can foster growth and development. Parents are encouraged to embrace this opportunity to advocate for their child, seeking out programs and resources that align with their child's individual needs.

As the diagnostic process unfolds, it is crucial for parents to educate themselves about autism and its spectrum. This knowledge empowers them to make informed decisions about therapies, educational settings, and support systems. In addition, it helps parents communicate effectively with educators and healthcare providers, ensuring that their child receives the best possible care. Workshops, support groups, and online resources can provide valuable insights and foster connections with others who share similar experiences.

Finally, the diagnostic journey is not just about identifying a condition; it is about embracing the unique qualities that each child brings to the world. Celebrating small victories, seeking joy in everyday moments, and fostering a nurturing environment are key to helping children on the spectrum flourish. As parents navigate the complexities of autism, they will find strength in their resilience and the love they impart. This journey, while challenging, is also filled with hope, growth, and the promise of a bright future for their children.

Importance Of Early Intervention

Early intervention plays a crucial role in the development of children on the autism spectrum. Research consistently shows that the earlier a child receives support, the more significant the benefits. Early intervention can lead to improved communication skills, enhanced social interactions, and greater independence as children grow. By addressing challenges and fostering strengths from a young age, parents and caregivers can help their children navigate the complexities of autism with greater confidence and resilience. This proactive approach lays the groundwork for lifelong skills that can empower children to thrive in various environments.

The importance of recognizing early signs of autism cannot be overstated. Parents and guardians are often the first to notice subtle differences in their child's behavior or development. By being attuned to these early indicators, such as difficulties in communication, challenges with social cues, or unusual play patterns, families can seek timely evaluations and interventions. Early diagnosis opens the door to tailored educational strategies that align with the child's unique needs, ensuring they receive the appropriate support to flourish academically and socially. This early engagement can pave the way for a more successful and fulfilling life.

Moreover, early intervention can have a ripple effect on the entire family unit. When parents access resources and support systems early, they become better equipped to understand their child's needs. This understanding fosters a nurturing environment where children feel secure and are encouraged to express themselves. Families can learn effective communication techniques and strategies to manage sensory sensitivities, ultimately creating a more harmonious home life. The emotional and psychological well-being of parents is equally vital; having access to support networks allows them to share experiences, gain insights, and feel less isolated in their journey.

In the context of educational strategies, early intervention provides a significant advantage. Tailored programs that incorporate individualized learning plans can help children develop essential skills that promote academic success. Schools that recognize the value of early intervention can implement inclusive practices that support children on the spectrum, fostering an environment where they can thrive alongside their peers. As children develop social skills and self-advocacy, they become more integrated into their communities, which enhances their ability to form meaningful relationships and participate fully in society.

Finally, embracing the concept of early intervention extends beyond individual families; it calls for a collective societal effort to raise awareness and advocate for resources dedicated to autism support. Communities that prioritize early intervention create a culture of understanding, acceptance, and inclusion. By working together, we can ensure that all children, regardless of their challenges, have the opportunity to realize their potential. The journey may be filled with obstacles, but with early intervention, families can foster hope and resilience, guiding their children toward a brighter future.

CHAPTER 3: EDUCATIONAL STRATEGIES FOR CHILDREN ON THE AUTISM SPECTRUM

Individualized Education Plans (Ieps)

Individualized Education Plans (IEPs) serve as a cornerstone for fostering the educational success of children with autism. These plans are tailored to meet the unique needs of each child, ensuring that their individual strengths and challenges are acknowledged and addressed. For parents and guardians, understanding the components of an IEP is essential in advocating for their child's right to a quality education. It is not just a document; it represents a commitment to supporting your child's learning journey in a way that resonates with their specific needs and aspirations.

Developing an IEP is a collaborative process that involves parents, educators, and specialists working together to create a roadmap for the child's educational experience. This partnership is vital, as it empowers parents to voice their concerns and insights about their child's abilities and challenges. By actively participating in the development of the IEP, parents can ensure that their child's goals are not only realistic but also inspiring. This collaboration fosters hope and encourages parents to envision a positive educational path for their children, reinforcing the belief that every child can thrive in an environment tailored just for them.

The IEP outlines specific educational goals, accommodations, and services that will support the child's learning. These goals are often aligned with the child's strengths, promoting engagement and motivation. For instance, if a child excels in visual learning, the IEP may include strategies that leverage this strength, such as using visual aids or hands-on activities. Additionally, accommodations might include sensory breaks or modified assignments, designed to create an inclusive environment where children can focus and participate fully. This personalized approach not only enhances educational outcomes but also nurtures a sense of belonging and self-worth within the classroom.

Beyond academics, IEPs address critical areas such as social skills development and sensory processing. These components are essential, as they help children navigate interactions with peers and manage sensory stimuli that may be overwhelming. By incorporating social skills training and sensory strategies into the IEP, parents and educators work together to equip children with the tools they need to succeed both in school and in their broader social environments. Such strategies pave the way for meaningful relationships and improved communication, laying a strong foundation for lifelong skills.

Finally, the IEP is a living document, subject to change as the child grows and their needs evolve. Regular reviews and updates ensure that the plan remains relevant and effective, providing ongoing support. For parents, this means staying engaged and informed, advocating for their child at every stage. By recognizing the IEP as a dynamic tool, parents can foster resilience and adaptability in their children, empowering them to face challenges with confidence. This journey through the IEP process not only enhances the educational experience for children with autism but also inspires parents to champion their child's potential, reinforcing the belief that every child deserves the opportunity to shine.

Classroom Accommodations

Classroom accommodations are essential for fostering an inclusive and supportive learning environment for children on the autism spectrum. These adjustments not only recognize the unique needs of each child but also empower them to thrive academically and socially. By implementing tailored strategies, educators can help children with autism navigate the complexities of the classroom, allowing their strengths to shine while providing the support they need to overcome challenges.

One of the most effective accommodations is the modification of teaching methods to incorporate diverse learning styles. Visual aids, hands-on activities, and interactive technology can make lessons more accessible and engaging for students with autism. By presenting information in various formats, educators can cater to the individual strengths of each child, promoting a deeper understanding of the material. This approach not only enhances learning but also builds confidence, encouraging students to participate more actively in their education.

Another critical aspect of classroom accommodations is creating a structured environment. Predictability and routine can significantly reduce anxiety for children on the spectrum. Teachers can establish clear schedules, use visual timetables, and provide advance notice of changes to the daily routine. These strategies help students feel secure and focused, enabling them to engage fully in their learning experience. Additionally, incorporating sensory-friendly spaces within the classroom allows students to take breaks when needed, ensuring they can return to their tasks feeling refreshed and ready to learn.

Social skills development is another vital component of classroom accommodations. Educators can facilitate opportunities for peer interactions through group work, buddy systems, and structured social skills lessons. These initiatives encourage children to practice communication and collaboration in a supportive setting. By fostering social connections, educators help build a sense of belonging and acceptance, which is crucial for the emotional well-being of children with autism. This nurturing environment can lead to lasting friendships that extend beyond the classroom.

Ultimately, classroom accommodations create a foundation for success that extends far beyond academics. By recognizing the unique strengths and challenges of children on the autism spectrum, educators and parents can collaborate to design an educational experience that is enriching and fulfilling. The journey may require patience and persistence, but the rewards of seeing a child thrive in a supportive environment are immeasurable. Together, we can create a world where every child has the opportunity to reach their full potential, fostering a brighter future for individuals with autism and society as a whole.

Collaborative Learning Approaches

Collaborative learning approaches offer a unique and enriching way to foster growth and development in children on the autism spectrum. By emphasizing teamwork and shared goals, these strategies create inclusive environments where children can thrive socially and academically. The essence of collaborative learning lies in its ability to celebrate diversity, allowing children to contribute their unique perspectives while learning from one another. Parents can take heart in knowing that these collaborative environments not only aid in knowledge acquisition but also enhance social skills, confidence, and a sense of belonging among peers.

In the classroom, teachers can implement collaborative learning techniques through group projects, peer mentoring, and cooperative games. These methods encourage children to work together towards a common objective, promoting communication and cooperation. For children on the autism spectrum, such interactions can be particularly beneficial, as they provide structured opportunities to practice social skills in a supportive setting. By engaging with their peers, children learn to navigate social cues, share ideas, and develop empathy, essential building blocks for meaningful relationships.

Outside of the classroom, families can further reinforce collaborative learning through community involvement and extracurricular activities. Programs that focus on teamwork, such as sports, art groups, or drama clubs, offer children a platform to connect with others who share similar interests. Parents can encourage their children to participate in these activities, supporting their growth while fostering friendships and social networks. These experiences not only enrich their lives but also help demystify autism for others, creating a more understanding and inclusive society.

Support for parents is a crucial aspect of collaborative learning approaches. By connecting with other families who share similar experiences, parents can exchange valuable insights, strategies, and emotional support. This sense of community can be incredibly empowering, as parents collaborate to advocate for their children's needs in educational settings and beyond. Workshops, support groups, and online forums can serve as vital resources, allowing parents to learn from one another while building a network of encouragement and solidarity.

Ultimately, the journey of collaborative learning is about creating a brighter future for children on the autism spectrum. By embracing these approaches, parents, educators, and community members can work together to cultivate environments where every child feels valued and understood. This collaboration not only benefits the children directly involved but also fosters a culture of acceptance and awareness within society, paving the way for a more inclusive world. Through shared efforts, we can help individuals on the autism spectrum navigate their paths with confidence, resilience, and joy.

CHAPTER 4: SUPPORT FOR PARENTS OF CHILDREN WITH AUTISM

Building A Support Network

Building a support network is essential for parents and guardians of children on the autism spectrum. This journey can often feel isolating, filled with unique challenges that require not only understanding but also a community of empathy and shared experiences. By connecting with others who are navigating similar paths, you can find strength, encouragement, and valuable resources. Building this network is not just a practical step; it is a powerful realization that you are not alone in this journey.

Start by reaching out to local autism organizations and support groups. These communities often host meetings, workshops, and events where you can connect with other families, share stories, and learn from one another. Engaging in these gatherings provides a platform to discuss your experiences and gain insights from those who have walked similar paths. The friendships and connections you forge can become invaluable sources of support, allowing you to celebrate victories and seek guidance during difficult times.

Online forums and social media groups can also play a crucial role in expanding your support network. These digital spaces allow for an exchange of ideas, resources, and personal stories without the constraints of geographical boundaries. Parents from around the world share strategies, advice, and encouragement, creating a rich tapestry of support that is just a click away. Whether you are looking for tips on sensory processing issues or educational strategies, these networks can offer a wealth of information tailored to your needs.

In addition to connecting with other parents, consider involving professionals who specialize in autism spectrum disorders. Therapists, educators, and healthcare providers can be valuable allies in your journey. They can provide insights into therapeutic approaches, educational strategies, and resources that can benefit your child. Building relationships with these professionals ensures that you have trusted experts to turn to for guidance, reinforcing your support network with a solid foundation of knowledge and experience.

As you cultivate this support network, remember the importance of advocacy and awareness. Your voice matters, and by sharing your experiences and insights, you can help foster a greater understanding of autism in your community. Engage in conversations that promote awareness and acceptance, encouraging others to join you in supporting those on the spectrum. Together, through shared experiences and collective advocacy, we can create an environment where individuals with autism are recognized, valued, and supported in every aspect of their lives.

Self-Care For Parents

Self-care for parents of children with autism is not just a necessity; it is a vital component of effective parenting and family well-being. The journey of raising a child on the spectrum can be filled with unique challenges that can easily lead to emotional and physical exhaustion. It is crucial for parents to prioritize their own health and well-being in order to provide the best support for their children. Engaging in self-care allows parents to recharge, enabling them to be more present and effective in their roles. By recognizing the importance of self-care, parents can cultivate resilience, patience, and a greater capacity for joy amidst the trials.

Finding time for oneself may seem daunting, especially in the midst of busy schedules and the demands of daily life. However, small, intentional moments of self-care can make a profound difference. Whether it's taking a short walk, indulging in a favorite hobby, or simply enjoying a quiet cup of tea, these moments of respite can help restore balance. Parents should also consider the significance of connecting with others who understand their experiences. Support groups, whether in-person or online, offer a space for sharing stories, exchanging strategies, and finding solace in the shared journey of parenting a child with autism.

Physical health is another critical aspect of self-care that parents often overlook. Regular exercise, a balanced diet, and adequate sleep are foundational elements that can enhance physical and mental well-being. Parents may find that engaging in physical activities with their child can be both fun and beneficial. This not only fosters bonding but also promotes a healthy lifestyle for the entire family. Mindfulness practices, such as yoga or meditation, can also be effective tools for managing stress and cultivating a positive mindset.

Emotional self-care is equally important. Parents should allow themselves to experience and express a wide range of feelings, from joy to frustration. Journaling, art, or music can serve as outlets for these emotions, providing a means of processing the complexities of their experiences. Seeking professional support, such as counseling or therapy, can also be invaluable. It creates a safe space to explore feelings, develop coping strategies, and reinforce a parent's sense of self-worth and purpose.

Ultimately, self-care is not a luxury; it is a necessity for parents navigating the spectrum. By prioritizing their own well-being, parents not only enhance their capacity to support their children but also model healthy behaviors for them. In doing so, they create a nurturing environment that fosters growth, understanding, and love. Remember, caring for oneself is an essential investment in the entire family's journey, paving the way for a brighter future for both parents and children on the spectrum.

Navigating Resources And Services

Navigating the myriad resources and services available for children on the autism spectrum can feel overwhelming, yet it is essential for fostering their growth and well-being. As parents and guardians, understanding where to find support and how to utilize these resources can empower you and your child. The journey begins with recognizing the early signs of autism, as this awareness allows you to seek timely intervention. Early diagnosis opens doors to specialized educational strategies tailored to your child's unique needs, ensuring they receive the support necessary for their development.

Accessing educational resources is a vital step in this journey. Many schools and community organizations offer programs specifically designed for children on the autism spectrum. These programs often incorporate individualized learning plans and sensory-friendly environments that cater to your child's learning style. As you navigate these options, remember to advocate for your child's needs, working collaboratively with educators to implement effective strategies that promote social skills development and academic achievement. Your involvement can make a significant difference in how these resources are utilized.

Support for parents is equally crucial in this process. Connecting with local and online communities can provide you with valuable insights and emotional support. Many organizations offer workshops, counseling, and peer support groups that not only educate but also foster a sense of belonging among families facing similar challenges. These connections can inspire resilience and provide practical strategies for handling everyday situations related to autism. Remember, you are not alone on this journey; sharing experiences with others can illuminate paths you may not have considered.

As your child grows, exploring therapeutic approaches becomes increasingly important. Various therapies, from occupational and speech therapy to social skills training, can significantly enhance your child's ability to navigate the world. Each child is unique, and understanding which therapies resonate best with your child will require patience and exploration. Keep an open mind and stay informed about the latest research and advancements in autism therapies to provide your child with the best opportunities for success.

Finally, as your child approaches adulthood, consider the resources available for employment and career development. Many organizations specialize in preparing individuals on the autism spectrum for the workforce, focusing on their strengths and interests. Equipping your child with the necessary skills and confidence to enter the job market is crucial for fostering independence and self-sufficiency. By advocating for awareness and acceptance in society, you contribute to creating an environment where individuals with autism can thrive, ensuring that they, too, can navigate their paths with hope and determination.

CHAPTER 5: SENSORY PROCESSING IN AUTISM

Understanding Sensory Processing

Understanding sensory processing is crucial for parents and guardians of children with autism, as it plays a significant role in how these children perceive and interact with the world around them. Sensory processing refers to the brain's ability to receive, interpret, and respond to sensory information from the environment. For many children on the autism spectrum, this process can be atypical, leading to heightened sensitivities or diminished responses to stimuli. Recognizing these differences is the first step in fostering a supportive environment that helps children navigate their experiences with greater ease and comfort.

Children with autism may experience sensory processing challenges in various ways. Some may be overwhelmed by loud noises, bright lights, or certain textures, while others may seek out sensory experiences, such as spinning or jumping. These responses are not merely quirks; they are integral parts of how these children make sense of their surroundings. As parents, understanding these reactions can empower you to advocate for your child's needs, whether it's creating a sensory-friendly space at home, working with educators to modify classroom environments, or collaborating with therapists to develop coping strategies.

Creating an understanding of sensory processing challenges allows you to better support your child in their daily life. It encourages you to observe and identify patterns in their behavior, which can provide insights into their sensory preferences and aversions. For example, if your child becomes anxious in crowded places, this knowledge can guide you in planning outings that are more manageable for them. By acknowledging and addressing their sensory needs, you can help your child build confidence and resilience as they navigate social situations and educational settings.

In addition to supporting your child, understanding sensory processing can foster greater empathy and awareness within your community. Sharing your insights with teachers, caregivers, and peers can create a more inclusive environment where everyone is encouraged to recognize and respect individual differences. This advocacy not only benefits your child but also contributes to a broader understanding of autism in society, paving the way for more effective support systems and resources for families facing similar challenges.

As you journey through the complexities of sensory processing and autism, remember that each child is unique. Embrace the opportunity to learn alongside your child, seeking resources, connecting with other parents, and engaging with professionals who can provide guidance. By nurturing your understanding of sensory processing, you are not only empowering your child but also enriching your family's experiences, enabling them to thrive in a world that recognizes and celebrates diversity.

Strategies For Sensory Regulation

Understanding sensory regulation is vital for parents and guardians of children on the autism spectrum. Sensory processing challenges can manifest in various ways, making it essential to identify the specific sensory needs of each child. By observing their reactions to different stimuli—whether it's bright lights, loud noises, or certain textures—parents can begin to uncover patterns that inform effective sensory regulation strategies. This journey of discovery not only supports the child's comfort but also fosters a deeper bond between parent and child, turning everyday moments into opportunities for growth and understanding.

One powerful strategy for sensory regulation involves creating a sensory-friendly environment. This can mean designating a specific area in the home that is calm and soothing, equipped with items that provide comfort and security, such as weighted blankets, noise-canceling headphones, or soft lighting. Parents can involve their children in this process, allowing them to choose elements that resonate with their unique preferences. The act of customizing their space empowers children and helps them develop a sense of control over their sensory experiences, ultimately reducing anxiety and promoting self-regulation.

Incorporating regular sensory breaks into daily routines can also be immensely beneficial. These breaks give children the opportunity to engage in activities that either stimulate or calm their senses, depending on their individual needs. For instance, a child might benefit from jumping on a trampoline or squeezing a stress ball to release pent-up energy, while another might find solace in quiet activities like reading or listening to calming music. By scheduling these breaks, parents not only help their children manage sensory overload but also teach them the importance of self-care and recognizing their own sensory needs.

Another effective strategy is to teach children mindfulness and relaxation techniques. Simple practices, such as deep breathing exercises or guided imagery, can empower children to cope with overwhelming situations. By practicing these techniques regularly, children learn to recognize the early signs of sensory distress and can take proactive steps to manage their feelings. Parents can model these techniques, making it a shared family experience that reinforces emotional regulation and resilience, ultimately fostering a more harmonious home environment.

Finally, collaboration with educators and therapists can enhance the effectiveness of sensory regulation strategies. By working together, parents, teachers, and therapists can develop a comprehensive plan that addresses the child's sensory needs in various settings. This holistic approach not only supports the child's development but also builds a community of understanding and support around them. As parents advocate for their children's sensory needs, they contribute to a broader awareness of autism and its spectrum, empowering not only their child but also others facing similar challenges. Embracing these strategies can lead to a more fulfilling life for children on the autism spectrum, where they can thrive and shine in their unique ways.

Creating A Sensory-Friendly Environment

Creating a sensory-friendly environment is an essential step in supporting children with autism and enhancing their quality of life. Each child on the spectrum experiences the world in unique ways, often with heightened sensitivities to sensory input such as sounds, lights, textures, and smells. By understanding these sensory processing differences, parents and guardians can take proactive measures to create spaces that feel safe and nurturing. This tailored environment not only minimizes stressors but also encourages exploration, learning, and social interaction.

One of the first considerations in developing a sensory-friendly environment is to assess the sensory needs of your child. Observe their reactions to various stimuli, noting what they find overwhelming or calming. This insight is invaluable. For example, if your child is sensitive to bright lights, consider using softer lighting or blackout curtains to reduce glare. Similarly, if loud noises are distressing, soundproofing the room or providing noise-canceling headphones can make a significant difference. Creating zones within the home for different activities—such as a quiet reading nook or a tactile play area—can also help in catering to diverse sensory needs.

Incorporating sensory-friendly materials can further enhance the environment. Textured fabrics, weighted blankets, and fidget tools can provide comfort and help alleviate anxiety. When selecting toys and materials, prioritize those that engage various senses without overwhelming them. Simple items like building blocks, sensory bins filled with rice or beans, and calming essential oils can transform a space into a sanctuary of exploration and creativity. Remember, the goal is to create a space that both comforts and engages your child, allowing them to thrive in their surroundings.

The organization of space plays a crucial role in sensory-friendly design. A cluttered environment can be overwhelming, making it difficult for children to focus and engage. By simplifying the layout and ensuring that items are easily accessible, you encourage independence and reduce anxiety. Use shelves and storage solutions to keep toys and materials organized, allowing your child to choose what they want to play with, fostering a sense of control and autonomy. Additionally, consider the placement of furniture to create open pathways that promote movement and exploration.

Ultimately, creating a sensory-friendly environment is about fostering acceptance and understanding. As parents and guardians, your efforts to design spaces that honor your child's sensory needs can have profound effects. Not only do these environments promote comfort and security, but they also empower children with autism to engage more fully with the world around them. By embracing the unique sensory profiles of your children, you are taking a powerful step in advocating for their well-being and helping them navigate their individual journeys with confidence and joy.

CHAPTER 6: SOCIAL SKILLS DEVELOPMENT FOR INDIVIDUALS WITH AUTISM

Importance Of Social Skills

Social skills are a vital component of human interaction, serving as the glue that binds individuals together within society. For children on the autism spectrum, developing these skills can pose unique challenges, yet it also offers a pathway to meaningful relationships and greater independence. Understanding the importance of social skills is crucial for parents and guardians, as it empowers them to support their children in navigating social landscapes with confidence, resilience, and joy. By fostering these skills, families can help their children not only connect with peers but also thrive in various social settings.

The foundation of social skills begins with communication. For many children with autism, expressive and receptive language can be areas of difficulty. However, fostering communication skills does not solely rely on verbal interactions; it encompasses non-verbal cues, body language, and even the use of technology. Parents can play a pivotal role in enhancing these skills by creating opportunities for dialogue, modeling effective communication techniques, and using visual aids or assistive devices when necessary. This active involvement not only aids in the development of social skills but also reinforces the child's sense of self-worth and belonging.

Equally important is the ability to interpret social cues, which can often be nuanced and complex. Children on the spectrum may find it challenging to understand facial expressions, tone of voice, and contextual clues. By engaging in role-playing activities or using social stories, parents can help their children practice recognizing and responding to these cues in a safe environment. This practice not only builds competence but also fosters empathy and emotional intelligence, essential traits for building lasting relationships. The joy of connection can be profound, and witnessing a child navigate social interactions with newfound skills can be an inspiring experience for the entire family.

Moreover, social skills play a crucial role in educational settings, where collaboration and peer interaction are often necessary for success. Encouraging participation in group activities, clubs, or team sports can provide children with valuable opportunities to practice their social skills in real-world scenarios. These experiences can lead to friendships and a sense of community, which are instrumental in promoting mental health and emotional well-being. Parents can advocate for inclusive educational environments that recognize and support the diverse social needs of their children, ensuring they have the tools and opportunities to flourish academically and socially.

Finally, as children with autism grow into adolescence and adulthood, the importance of social skills extends to employment and career development. The ability to work collaboratively, communicate effectively, and build professional relationships can open doors to fulfilling job opportunities. Parents can guide their children in developing these skills by facilitating internships, volunteering, or job shadowing experiences. By nurturing social competencies, families can help their children not only envision a brighter future but also step into it with confidence, knowing they possess the skills necessary to navigate the world around them. Embracing the journey of social skills development can lead to a life filled with connection, purpose, and joy.

Teaching Social Skills

Teaching social skills to children with autism is a journey that requires patience, creativity, and understanding. Social interactions can be challenging for children on the spectrum, often leading to feelings of frustration or isolation. However, with the right strategies and support, parents and guardians can help their children develop essential social skills that will enable them to connect with others and navigate various social situations. It is important to recognize that every child progresses at their own pace, and celebrating small victories along the way can greatly enhance their confidence and motivation.

One of the most effective ways to teach social skills is through modeling and role-playing. Children learn by observing the behaviors of those around them, and parents can set examples by demonstrating appropriate social interactions in real-life situations. Engaging in role-play scenarios allows children to practice these interactions in a safe environment. For instance, parents can create situations that involve greetings, sharing, or asking for help, guiding their child in how to respond appropriately. This technique not only reinforces learning but also encourages children to express their feelings and understand those of others.

Incorporating visual supports can also enhance social skills development for children with autism. Visual schedules, social stories, and picture cards can help clarify social expectations and appropriate responses. These tools provide concrete examples of social interactions, making it easier for children to grasp abstract concepts. Parents can use these visuals to illustrate specific scenarios, such as making eye contact during conversations or recognizing when someone is upset. By breaking down these interactions into manageable steps, children can approach social situations with greater understanding and confidence.

Creating opportunities for social interactions is vital in promoting social skills. Parents can facilitate playdates, group activities, or community events where their children can interact with peers in a structured setting. Participating in activities that align with their interests, such as sports, art classes, or clubs, can also encourage children to connect with others who share similar passions. These experiences not only provide practical social skills practice but also help children build friendships and develop a sense of belonging, which is crucial for their emotional well-being.

Finally, fostering an environment of acceptance and encouragement at home can significantly impact a child's social skills development. Parents should celebrate their child's efforts and progress, no matter how small, reinforcing the idea that making mistakes is a natural part of learning. Open communication about social experiences, both positive and negative, allows children to reflect on their interactions and understand different perspectives. With love, support, and appropriate guidance, parents can empower their children to navigate the complexities of social relationships, paving the way for a brighter, more connected future.

Role-Playing And Social Stories

Role-playing and social stories are powerful tools that can significantly enhance the social skills of children on the autism spectrum. These techniques offer structured opportunities for children to practice interactions in a safe and supportive environment. By simulating real-life scenarios, role-playing allows children to explore various social situations, understand different perspectives, and develop the confidence needed to navigate their social worlds. Parents and guardians can facilitate these activities at home, empowering their children to express themselves, share their feelings, and learn appropriate responses in a way that feels both engaging and relevant to their everyday lives.

Incorporating role-playing into daily routines can be as simple as using familiar settings, like a grocery store or a playground, to create scenarios that mimic real-life interactions. Parents can take turns acting out different roles, whether it's a customer and a cashier or friends meeting at the park. This not only helps children practice verbal communication but also emphasizes non-verbal cues, such as body language and facial expressions. By breaking down complex social exchanges into manageable parts, children can gradually build their understanding and comfort level, making the process both enjoyable and educational.

Social stories complement role-playing by providing children with clear, concise narratives that outline social situations and expected behaviors. These stories can address a wide range of scenarios, from starting a conversation to coping with unexpected changes in routine. By reading and discussing social stories, parents can help their children visualize what to expect in various situations, reducing anxiety and promoting a sense of readiness. The use of simple language and illustrations can enhance comprehension, allowing children to internalize the lessons and apply them in real-life contexts.

As children engage with role-playing and social stories, they begin to develop essential social skills that extend beyond the immediate activities. These skills, which include turn-taking, sharing, and understanding social cues, are foundational for building friendships and fostering meaningful relationships. Moreover, the confidence gained from repeated practice can lead to greater participation in group activities, enhancing their overall sense of belonging and acceptance within their communities. Parents play a crucial role in reinforcing these skills through ongoing encouragement and positive reinforcement.

Ultimately, the integration of role-playing and social stories into the lives of children with autism is a journey of growth and discovery. It fosters not only the development of social skills but also a deeper understanding of themselves and their interactions with others. By embracing these techniques, parents and guardians can create a nurturing environment that celebrates their child's uniqueness while equipping them with the tools they need to thrive socially. This supportive approach cultivates resilience and empowers children on the spectrum to navigate their social landscapes with confidence and joy.

CHAPTER 7: EMPLOYMENT AND CAREER DEVELOPMENT FOR ADULTS ON THE AUTISM SPECTRUM

Preparing For The Workforce

Preparing for the workforce is a crucial milestone for individuals on the autism spectrum, and as parents or guardians, your role in this journey is vital. Understanding the unique strengths and challenges your child may face in the job market can empower you to provide the right support and guidance. By fostering an environment that emphasizes their interests and talents, you can help your child develop the confidence and skills needed to navigate the complexities of employment. This preparation starts with recognizing their individual abilities and passions, which can lead to fulfilling career paths that resonate with who they are.

Encouraging practical experiences, such as internships or volunteer work, can be incredibly beneficial. These opportunities allow your child to explore various fields while gaining essential skills in a real-world setting. It's important to advocate for inclusive programs that cater to their specific needs, ensuring a supportive atmosphere. Building social skills in these environments can also enhance their ability to interact with peers and supervisors, paving the way for a successful transition into the workforce. Remember, every experience counts, and each step taken can lead to greater independence.

Education plays a pivotal role in preparing individuals for employment. Collaborate with educators to create personalized learning plans that focus on both academic and vocational skills. Many schools offer programs tailored to help students with autism develop employability skills, such as teamwork, communication, and problem-solving. Engaging in these educational strategies can help bridge the gap between academics and the workforce. As your child progresses, encourage them to pursue subjects that align with their interests and strengths, fostering a sense of ownership over their educational journey.

As your child approaches adulthood, discussions about career aspirations should become increasingly frequent. Encouraging open conversations about their goals, fears, and interests can help them envision their future. Providing information on various career options, including those that prioritize their strengths, will empower them to make informed decisions. It's essential to instill a sense of optimism and resilience, reminding them that setbacks are a natural part of any journey. Celebrate their achievements, no matter how small, as this will reinforce their self-esteem and motivation.

Ultimately, the journey to workforce readiness is a collaborative effort that involves parents, educators, and the community. By advocating for resources, creating opportunities, and nurturing your child's unique abilities, you can significantly impact their success. Emphasizing the importance of perseverance, adaptability, and lifelong learning will equip them with the tools necessary to thrive in a competitive job market. With your unwavering support and belief in their potential, your child can navigate the workforce with confidence, ready to contribute their unique perspectives and talents to the world.

Finding Suitable Employment

Finding suitable employment for individuals on the autism spectrum is a crucial step toward independence and self-fulfillment. It is essential for parents and guardians to recognize that each individual possesses unique strengths and talents that can be harnessed in the workplace. By focusing on these attributes, parents can help their children explore career paths that align with their interests and abilities. Encouragement and support from family members can empower individuals to envision a future where they can thrive professionally, contributing meaningfully to society.

Understanding the specific needs and preferences of a child with autism is vital in guiding them toward suitable employment.

This process may involve identifying their interests, skills, and sensory requirements, which can influence the type of work environment they may flourish in. For instance, some individuals may excel in structured settings with clear routines, while others might thrive in creative or flexible environments. By engaging in open conversations about their aspirations, parents can foster an atmosphere of trust and understanding, helping their children articulate their goals and preferences.

Networking and building connections within the community can also play a significant role in finding suitable employment. Parents can assist their children in developing relationships with mentors, peers, and potential employers who value diversity and inclusivity. Participating in job fairs, community events, and workshops tailored for individuals on the spectrum can create opportunities for meaningful interactions and potential employment leads. By advocating for their children within these spaces, parents can raise awareness about the capabilities of individuals with autism and promote their strengths to prospective employers.

Moreover, it is essential for parents to be well-informed about available resources that can assist their children in their job search. Various organizations and programs offer vocational training, job coaching, and employment support specifically designed for individuals with autism. These resources can help bridge the gap between education and employment, equipping individuals with the skills they need to succeed in the workforce. Encouraging participation in these programs can enhance confidence and prepare individuals for the challenges and intricacies of job hunting and workplace dynamics.

Finally, celebrating small successes along the employment journey is vital for maintaining motivation and resilience. Whether landing an interview, completing a job training program, or receiving positive feedback from a potential employer, acknowledging these milestones helps foster a positive outlook on the future. Parents can play a key role in this process by emphasizing the importance of perseverance and adaptability. By instilling a growth mindset and reinforcing the belief that setbacks can lead to valuable learning experiences, parents can guide their children toward finding fulfilling employment that not only supports their independence but also enriches their lives and the lives of those around them.

Workplace Accommodations And Support

Workplace accommodations and support are essential components in fostering an inclusive environment for individuals on the autism spectrum. As parents and guardians, understanding the significance of these accommodations can empower you to advocate for your child's needs as they transition into the workforce. The workplace can often be overwhelming, presenting sensory challenges, social expectations, and communication barriers. However, with the right support systems in place, individuals with autism can thrive and contribute their unique talents and perspectives.

Employers who implement thoughtful accommodations demonstrate a commitment to diversity and inclusion, creating a culture where everyone can succeed. Simple adjustments, such as flexible work hours, quiet workspaces, or clear communication protocols, can make a profound difference in the daily experiences of employees on the spectrum. These accommodations not only help mitigate potential stressors but also promote a sense of belonging and confidence that can lead to increased productivity and job satisfaction.

In addition to physical adjustments, providing access to support resources is crucial. Mentorship programs, training sessions on workplace etiquette, and social skills workshops can equip individuals with essential tools to navigate their roles effectively. Encouraging open communication about individual needs and preferences can also foster a supportive atmosphere where employees feel safe to express their concerns or request assistance. This proactive approach not only benefits the individual but also enriches the entire team by enhancing collaboration and understanding.

As a parent, you play a vital role in preparing your child for these workplace experiences. Engaging in conversations about their strengths, interests, and potential challenges can help them develop self-advocacy skills. Encouraging your child to practice job interviews, build professional relationships, and explore their passions will empower them to approach the workforce with confidence. By instilling these values, you set the stage for your child to seek out environments that celebrate their unique contributions.

Ultimately, fostering awareness and advocacy for workplace accommodations is a collective effort that requires the engagement of parents, employers, and society. By working together to create inclusive spaces, we can dismantle barriers and pave the way for a brighter future for individuals on the autism spectrum. Embracing their strengths and providing the necessary support will not only help them realize their potential but also enrich the workplaces and communities they become a part of, leading to a more compassionate and diverse society.

CHAPTER 8: THERAPEUTIC APPROACHES FOR AUTISM SPECTRUM DISORDERS

Overview Of Therapeutic Options

In the journey of understanding and supporting a child with Autism, it is essential to explore the diverse therapeutic options available. These approaches can significantly enhance a child's quality of life, fostering their growth and development in various domains. From early intervention strategies to ongoing support as they transition into adulthood, the therapeutic landscape is rich with possibilities that empower both the child and their family. Each therapeutic option is a stepping stone toward unlocking a child's potential and creating a brighter future.

One of the most widely recognized therapeutic approaches is Applied Behavior Analysis (ABA). This evidence-based method focuses on reinforcing positive behaviors while minimizing those that may be challenging. ABA is tailored to meet the unique needs of each child, ensuring that therapy is both effective and engaging. By breaking down tasks into manageable steps, children can achieve milestones that build their confidence and skills. The beauty of ABA lies in its adaptability; it can be applied in various settings, including home, school, and community environments, making it a versatile tool in a parent's toolkit.

In addition to ABA, speech and language therapy plays a crucial role in helping children with Autism communicate more effectively. Many children on the spectrum experience difficulties with verbal and non-verbal communication. Speech therapists employ a range of techniques to enhance language skills, social communication, and articulation. This support not only fosters better interaction with peers and family members but also contributes to a child's overall self-expression and emotional well-being. As parents, witnessing improvements in communication can be a powerful motivator and source of hope.

Occupational therapy is another vital component of a comprehensive therapeutic plan. It focuses on developing the skills necessary for daily living, such as self-care, play, and social interaction. Occupational therapists often incorporate sensory integration techniques to help children process sensory information more effectively, reducing anxiety and promoting comfort in various situations. These skills are essential as children navigate their environments, allowing them to participate more fully in activities they enjoy and engage more meaningfully with those around them.

As children grow, therapeutic options continue to evolve, addressing their changing needs. Social skills training, for instance, becomes increasingly important as children transition into adolescence and adulthood. Programs designed to enhance social interactions can help individuals on the spectrum build meaningful relationships and improve their ability to navigate complex social situations. Furthermore, exploring vocational training and employment support for adults with Autism opens doors to independence and fulfillment. By embracing a wide array of therapeutic options, parents can guide their children on a path toward a successful and enriched life, celebrating each small victory along the way.

Behavioral Therapy Techniques

Behavioral therapy techniques play a pivotal role in supporting children with autism spectrum disorder, empowering them to navigate their unique challenges and thrive in their environments. These techniques are grounded in the principles of applied behavior analysis (ABA), which focus on understanding how behavior is shaped by interactions with the environment. For parents and guardians, this means that by observing and interpreting their child's behaviors, they can implement strategies that foster positive changes, enhancing communication, social skills, and daily living activities. Embracing these techniques can transform the way families engage with their children, nurturing their growth and development in profound ways.

One of the most effective behavioral therapy techniques is

reinforcement, which involves encouraging desired behaviors through rewards. This approach can be particularly beneficial in promoting communication and social interactions. For instance, when a child expresses a need or desire verbally, providing positive reinforcement—like praise or a small reward—can motivate them to continue using words instead of gestures. This technique not only fosters language development but also builds the child's confidence in their ability to communicate effectively. Parents can create a structured environment where these opportunities for reinforcement are abundant, turning everyday moments into valuable learning experiences.

Another essential technique is modeling, where adults demonstrate appropriate behaviors for children to emulate. This method is especially significant when teaching social skills, as children with autism often benefit from visual and practical examples. Parents can role-play different social scenarios, such as greeting a friend or sharing toys, allowing their child to observe and practice these interactions in a safe setting. By providing clear demonstrations and gentle guidance, parents help their children internalize these skills, making real-world interactions less daunting. This proactive approach not only equips children with essential tools for social engagement but also fosters a sense of belonging and acceptance in various social contexts.

Additionally, the technique of prompting is invaluable for encouraging specific behaviors. Prompts can be verbal, visual, or physical cues that guide children toward the desired actions. For example, if a child struggles to initiate a conversation, a parent might use a visual cue, like a picture of a friend, to remind the child to say hello. Gradually fading these prompts as the child becomes more independent is crucial, as it helps build their confidence and self-reliance. This technique instills a sense of achievement as children learn to navigate social situations without relying on external cues, reinforcing their ability to engage meaningfully with peers and adults alike.

Finally, the incorporation of visual supports, such as schedules and charts, can significantly enhance comprehension and routine adherence for children on the autism spectrum. These tools provide visual representations of daily activities, helping children understand what to expect and reducing anxiety associated with transitions. By creating a predictable environment, parents can enable their children to thrive, allowing them to focus on developing essential skills rather than feeling overwhelmed by uncertainty. Embracing these behavioral therapy techniques not only empowers children with autism but also strengthens the bond between parents and their children, fostering a nurturing environment where growth and learning can flourish.

Complementary Therapies

Complementary therapies offer a holistic approach to supporting children on the autism spectrum, emphasizing the importance of treating the whole person rather than just specific symptoms. For parents and guardians, exploring these therapies can be a transformative journey, providing additional tools to enhance their child's well-being and development. Whether it's through mindfulness practices, art therapy, or animal-assisted therapy, these modalities can foster emotional growth, improve communication skills, and create a sense of connection that is often essential for children with autism.

One of the most accessible complementary therapies is mindfulness and meditation. These practices encourage children to develop self-awareness and emotional regulation, which can be particularly beneficial for those who struggle with anxiety or sensory overload. By cultivating a calm and focused mind, children can better navigate social situations and engage more fully in their educational environments. Parents can participate alongside their children, creating shared experiences that strengthen their bond and provide valuable tools for managing daily challenges.

Art therapy is another powerful complementary approach that allows children to express themselves in non-verbal ways. For many on the spectrum, traditional communication can be a barrier, making it difficult to convey thoughts and feelings. Through painting, sculpting, or other creative outlets, children can explore their emotions and communicate experiences that may otherwise remain unspoken. This form of therapy not only nurtures creativity but also fosters a sense of accomplishment and boosts self-esteem, helping children to see themselves as capable and unique individuals.

Animal-assisted therapy introduces a gentle and nurturing element into therapeutic practices. Interactions with animals can provide comfort and reduce anxiety, offering children a safe space to explore their feelings. The unconditional love and companionship that animals provide can enhance social skills, as children learn to communicate and connect with their furry friends. Moreover, these experiences can be incredibly grounding, helping children to develop empathy and understanding—qualities that are essential for building relationships with peers and family members.

As parents and guardians navigate the complexities of autism, incorporating complementary therapies into their child's routine can be incredibly beneficial. These approaches not only support therapeutic goals but also create joyful moments that enrich family life. By embracing a diverse range of therapies, families can foster resilience, creativity, and connection, ultimately empowering their children to thrive on their unique journeys through life. The integration of complementary therapies into the care plan is a testament to the belief that every child has the potential to flourish, inspiring communities to understand and celebrate the diverse spectrum of autism.

CHAPTER 9: AUTISM AND CO OCCURRING CONDITIONS

Understanding Co-Occurring Conditions

As parents and guardians of children on the autism spectrum, it is crucial to recognize that autism often coexists with a variety of other conditions that can impact your child's overall well-being. These co-occurring conditions, which may include anxiety disorders, attention-deficit/hyperactivity disorder (ADHD), sensory processing disorders, and learning disabilities, can present unique challenges. Understanding these conditions can empower you to advocate effectively for your child, ensuring they receive comprehensive support tailored to their individual needs. Embracing this knowledge can illuminate the path forward, fostering resilience and growth for both you and your child.

The interplay between autism and co-occurring conditions can sometimes complicate the diagnosis and treatment process. Symptoms of these additional conditions may overlap with those of autism, making it essential for parents to be observant and informed. For instance, a child with autism may also experience heightened anxiety in social situations, which can amplify feelings of isolation and frustration. By acknowledging these co-occurring conditions, you can work closely with healthcare professionals to develop a holistic approach to your child's care, ensuring that all aspects of their health are considered and addressed.

Educational settings play a significant role in supporting children with autism and co-occurring conditions. Tailored educational strategies can make a world of difference in helping your child thrive academically and socially. Collaborating with teachers and school staff to implement individualized education plans (IEPs) and to foster an inclusive classroom environment is vital. By integrating strategies that address both autism and any additional challenges, you can help your child build essential skills and confidence, paving the way for a brighter future.

The emotional toll of navigating co-occurring conditions can be substantial for both children and their families. As a parent, seeking support for yourself is just as important as advocating for your child. Connecting with other parents who share similar experiences can provide invaluable insights and encouragement. Additionally, accessing resources such as therapy, support groups, and community programs can equip you with the tools needed to foster resilience within your family. Remember, you are not alone in this journey; there is a vast network of support ready to uplift and inspire you.

Ultimately, understanding co-occurring conditions is about embracing the complexities of your child's experience and recognizing their unique strengths. By fostering an open dialogue about these conditions, you can empower your child to develop self-awareness and advocate for their needs. With love, patience, and informed guidance, you can help your child navigate life's challenges, transforming potential obstacles into stepping stones for growth and success. Together, you can create a future filled with hope, understanding, and endless possibilities.

Strategies For Integrated Support

In the journey of supporting a child with autism, integrating various strategies can create a harmonious environment that nurtures their development. One of the most effective approaches is to foster collaboration among educators, therapists, and family members. This collaborative effort ensures that everyone involved in the child's life is on the same page, sharing insights and strategies that can be tailored to meet the unique needs of the child. By establishing regular communication channels, whether through meetings, phone calls, or digital platforms, parents can cultivate a robust support network that promotes consistency and understanding across different settings.

Another vital strategy is the establishment of structured routines that provide predictability and security for children on the autism spectrum. Routines help reduce anxiety and can be especially beneficial for children who may struggle with transitions. Parents can work with educators to implement similar schedules at school and home, allowing the child to feel a sense of stability regardless of the environment. Visual schedules and timers can be powerful tools in reinforcing these routines, offering children clear expectations and promoting their ability to navigate daily activities with confidence.

Social skills development is an essential aspect of integrated support. Engaging children in social skills groups can provide a safe space for them to practice interactions with peers, guided by trained facilitators. These groups can focus on specific areas, such as understanding social cues, initiating conversations, and managing conflicts. Parents can also play a pivotal role by modeling social interactions at home and encouraging playdates with neurotypical peers. By fostering these connections, children can learn valuable skills that will serve them throughout their lives, laying the groundwork for meaningful relationships.

Sensory processing is another critical area that requires integrated support strategies. Many children with autism experience sensory sensitivities that can impact their ability to engage in daily activities. Parents and educators can work together to identify sensory triggers and create sensory-friendly environments. This may involve providing sensory breaks throughout the day or incorporating calming sensory activities into routines. By addressing sensory needs, parents can help their children feel more comfortable and focused, ultimately enhancing their overall learning and social experiences.

Lastly, advocacy and awareness play a crucial role in creating an inclusive society for individuals on the autism spectrum. Parents and guardians can become powerful voices in their communities, promoting understanding and acceptance of autism. By sharing their experiences and advocating for appropriate resources and support systems, they can help pave the way for future generations. Together, families can collaborate with local organizations, schools, and policymakers to build a more inclusive world, where every child has the opportunity to thrive and reach their full potential.

Resources For Co-Occurring Conditions

Navigating the challenges that accompany autism can often reveal a landscape of co-occurring conditions that may affect your child's development and well-being. Understanding these conditions is essential for parents, as they can provide context and clarity in navigating the complex journey of autism. Co-occurring conditions, such as anxiety, ADHD, sensory processing disorders, and learning disabilities, are not uncommon among children on the autism spectrum. Recognizing their presence and understanding their implications can empower you to advocate effectively for your child's needs, ensuring they receive the comprehensive support necessary to thrive.

One of the most valuable resources available to parents is access to specialized healthcare professionals who can provide assessments and tailored interventions. Pediatricians, psychologists, and speech therapists can help identify co-occurring conditions early on, allowing you to develop an individualized plan that addresses all aspects of your child's development. This collaboration is crucial, as it fosters a holistic approach to care that encompasses not only autism but also any additional challenges your child may face. By engaging with these professionals, you can create a support network that is both informed and compassionate, guiding your child toward a brighter future.

In addition to professional help, there are numerous community resources and support groups designed to assist families navigating these complexities. Local and national organizations often offer workshops, informational resources, and peer support networks that can be invaluable. Connecting with other parents who share similar experiences can provide comfort and insight, as well as practical strategies for managing co-occurring conditions. These connections can remind you that you are not alone on this journey and that there is a community ready to offer understanding and encouragement.

Educational strategies play a pivotal role in addressing co-occurring conditions. Schools equipped with special education resources and trained staff can provide interventions tailored to your child's unique needs. Collaborating with educators to create an Individualized Education Program (IEP) that considers both autism and any co-occurring conditions is essential. This partnership can ensure your child has access to the tools and support necessary for academic success and social development. By fostering an inclusive educational environment, you can help your child build confidence and skills that will serve them throughout their life.

Ultimately, the journey of parenting a child with autism and co-occurring conditions is filled with challenges, yet it is also rich with opportunities for growth and understanding. By utilizing the resources available, connecting with professionals and peers, and advocating for your child's comprehensive needs, you can create a nurturing environment that allows your child to flourish. Remember, every step taken toward understanding and support is a step toward unlocking your child's full potential, paving the way for a fulfilling life filled with hope, connection, and joy.

CHAPTER 10: ADVOCACY AND AWARENESS FOR AUTISM SPECTRUM DISORDERS

The Role Of Advocacy

Advocacy plays a crucial role in the lives of children with autism and their families. It empowers parents and guardians to become active participants in navigating the complexities of the autism spectrum. By understanding the needs of their children and the challenges they face, parents can advocate effectively for the resources, support, and services necessary for their development. Advocacy is not just a responsibility; it is a journey that fosters resilience, confidence, and hope in the face of uncertainty. When parents step into the role of advocates, they not only support their own children but also contribute to a broader movement that strives for acceptance and understanding within society.

One of the most significant aspects of advocacy is raising awareness about autism and its spectrum. By sharing their experiences and knowledge, parents can help dispel myths, reduce stigma, and promote a more inclusive environment for children with autism. Awareness campaigns can take many forms, from community events to social media outreach, all aimed at educating the public about the unique strengths and challenges faced by individuals on the spectrum. As more people become informed, they are more likely to foster acceptance and support, creating a world where children with autism can thrive.

In addition to awareness, advocacy involves actively seeking out and securing necessary resources for children with autism. This may include educational accommodations, therapeutic services, or support programs tailored to their needs. Parents who advocate for their children often find themselves navigating the educational system, negotiating Individualized Education Programs (IEPs), and collaborating with teachers and administrators. By understanding their rights and the available resources, parents can ensure that their children receive the appropriate interventions that facilitate learning and growth. This proactive approach not only benefits the child but also strengthens the family's ability to face challenges together.

Social skills development is another critical area where advocacy can make a significant impact. Parents and guardians can advocate for social skills training programs that promote meaningful interactions and friendships for their children. These programs can provide essential tools for navigating social situations, helping children build confidence and improve their ability to connect with others. By championing the importance of social skills development, parents not only enhance their child's quality of life but also encourage a culture of understanding and empathy among peers.

Ultimately, advocacy is about creating a supportive community for individuals with autism and their families. By joining forces with other parents, educators, and advocates, families can amplify their voices and create lasting change. This collective effort fosters an environment where individuals with autism are recognized for their potential, celebrated for their uniqueness, and given the opportunities they deserve. Through advocacy, parents not only uplift their own children but also contribute to a brighter, more inclusive future for all those on the autism spectrum.

Raising Awareness In The Community

Raising awareness in the community is a vital step in fostering understanding and acceptance of autism. As parents and guardians, you hold the power to illuminate the unique gifts and challenges that come with autism spectrum disorders. By sharing your experiences and insights, you can help dispel myths and misconceptions that often surround autism. This journey begins at home, where open conversations about autism can empower your child and encourage others to embrace differences. Your voice can inspire change, guiding society toward a more inclusive environment where every individual is valued and understood.

Community engagement is essential in creating a supportive landscape for children with autism. Organizing local events, workshops, or information sessions can be an effective way to educate others. Collaborating with schools, community centers, and local organizations can amplify your efforts. These gatherings provide opportunities for parents to connect with educators and professionals who specialize in autism, fostering a network of support and shared knowledge. As you bring people together, you lay the groundwork for a community that understands and celebrates the diversity within the autism spectrum.

It is crucial to highlight the importance of early diagnosis and intervention. By raising awareness about the early signs of autism, you can empower other parents to seek help sooner, leading to more effective support for their children. Sharing stories of personal experiences can resonate deeply and encourage proactive measures in seeking resources. When communities become informed about the benefits of early intervention, they not only support affected families but also contribute to the overall development of children with autism. This collective understanding can significantly improve outcomes and provide children with the tools they need to thrive.

Social skills development is another area where community awareness plays a pivotal role. It is essential to create spaces where children on the spectrum can practice and enhance their social interactions. Initiatives such as inclusive playgroups or social skills workshops can bridge gaps between children with autism and their neurotypical peers. This not only fosters friendships but also helps demystify autism for those who may not have personal experience with it. Communities that prioritize social inclusion pave the way for a more empathetic society, where understanding and compassion are at the forefront of interactions.

Finally, advocacy is a powerful tool in raising awareness and promoting change. Encourage your community members to become vocal advocates for individuals with autism, whether through local legislation, education initiatives, or broader awareness campaigns. Your efforts can inspire others to join the cause, creating a ripple effect that reaches far beyond your immediate surroundings. By fostering a culture of advocacy, you contribute to a future where individuals on the autism spectrum are recognized for their potential and supported in their journey toward independence and fulfillment. Together, as a united community, you can champion awareness and create lasting, positive change for all.

Empowering Families And Individuals

Empowering families and individuals touched by autism is a journey that begins with understanding the unique characteristics of the spectrum. Each child with autism possesses distinct strengths and challenges, and recognizing these differences is the first step in fostering a supportive environment. By embracing the individuality of their children, parents can develop tailored strategies that resonate with their child's specific needs. This empowerment not only enhances the child's development but also strengthens the family unit, creating a nurturing space where growth and learning thrive.

Early signs and diagnosis of autism can often feel overwhelming for families. However, understanding these signs is crucial in accessing the right support and interventions. Parents should be encouraged to trust their instincts and seek professional guidance when they notice developmental differences. Early intervention has proven to be one of the most effective tools in supporting children on the spectrum. By acting swiftly, families can provide their children with the resources they need to flourish, setting the stage for a brighter future filled with possibilities.

Educational strategies play a vital role in empowering children on the autism spectrum. Schools and educators are increasingly recognizing the value of inclusive practices that celebrate diversity in learning styles. Parents can advocate for their children's educational needs, ensuring they receive personalized support that fosters both academic and social skills. By collaborating with teachers and special education professionals, families can create an educational environment where children not only succeed academically but also develop essential life skills that will serve them well beyond the classroom.

Support for parents of children with autism is equally important in this journey. The emotional and practical challenges faced by these families can be significant, but they are not alone. Building a strong network of support, whether through local community groups, online forums, or professional counseling, can provide crucial respite and resources. Sharing experiences with others who understand the unique challenges of parenting a child on the spectrum can offer strength and encouragement. This shared journey can inspire resilience and foster a sense of belonging among families navigating similar paths.

As individuals with autism grow into adulthood, empowerment continues to be paramount. Fostering independence and self-advocacy skills equips them to navigate the complexities of life beyond school. Employment and career development initiatives tailored for adults on the spectrum can open doors to fulfilling opportunities, encouraging the belief that they can contribute meaningfully to society. With the right tools and support, individuals with autism can achieve their dreams and inspire others, proving that empowerment is not just about overcoming challenges but also about celebrating strengths and potential.

CHAPTER 11: TECHNOLOGY AND TOOLS FOR SUPPORTING INDIVIDUALS WITH AUTISM

Assistive Technology Options

Assistive technology offers a remarkable array of tools designed to empower children on the autism spectrum, enhancing their communication, learning, and daily living skills. For parents and guardians, understanding these options can be transformative, providing valuable resources to support their child's unique needs. From simple tools to sophisticated devices, assistive technology can bridge communication gaps, foster independence, and encourage social interactions, making it an essential component in the toolkit for navigating autism.

Communication devices are among the most impactful assistive technologies available for children with autism. Augmentative and alternative communication (AAC) systems, including speech-generating devices and apps, empower non-verbal or minimally verbal children to express their thoughts and feelings. These tools can facilitate meaningful interactions and reduce frustration, helping children to engage more fully with their families and peers. By utilizing visual supports and symbols, AAC systems not only enhance communication but also encourage language development, allowing children to navigate their world more confidently.

In the realm of education, assistive technology plays a pivotal role in tailoring learning experiences to meet each child's individual needs. Tools such as interactive software, educational apps, and adaptive learning platforms can make lessons more engaging and accessible. These technologies can provide personalized feedback, helping children grasp concepts at their own pace. Moreover, visual schedules and organizational apps can support executive functioning skills, aiding children in managing tasks and routines effectively. Such resources empower parents to create enriching educational environments that celebrate their child's unique learning style.

Sensory processing challenges are common among children with autism, and assistive technology can help address these needs. Wearable devices that monitor sensory inputs or provide calming feedback can assist children in navigating overwhelming environments. Additionally, sensory-friendly apps and virtual reality experiences can offer safe spaces for exploration and relaxation. By integrating these technologies into daily routines, parents can foster a sense of security and well-being, ultimately enhancing their child's overall quality of life.

Finally, as children transition into adolescence and adulthood, assistive technology continues to play a crucial role in promoting independence and career development. Tools designed for job training, time management, and social skills development can equip young adults with the skills they need to thrive in the workforce. By advocating for the integration of these technologies in educational and vocational settings, parents can support their children's aspirations and help them navigate the challenges of adulthood. Embracing assistive technology not only empowers individuals on the autism spectrum but also inspires families and communities to foster inclusivity and understanding.

Apps And Software For Learning

In today's digital age, technology plays a pivotal role in enhancing the learning experience for children on the autism spectrum. The right apps and software can provide tailored educational opportunities that cater to individual learning styles, making it easier for children to engage with concepts at their own pace. These digital tools not only foster academic skills but also promote social interaction, emotional regulation, and sensory processing, paving the way for holistic development. For parents and guardians, understanding how to integrate these resources into their child's daily routine can open doors to new learning experiences and growth.

Numerous educational apps are specifically designed to address the unique challenges faced by children with autism. Many of these applications focus on building essential skills such as communication, social interaction, and daily living tasks. For example, apps that use visual schedules or social stories can help children understand routines and social cues, reducing anxiety and fostering independence. By utilizing these tools, parents can create a structured environment that enhances their child's ability to learn and thrive, making everyday activities more manageable and enjoyable.

Furthermore, technology can also support sensory processing needs. Many children on the autism spectrum experience sensory sensitivities that can impede their learning. Software that incorporates calming sounds, visual aids, or interactive elements can help create a sensory-friendly learning environment. These apps often allow customization, enabling parents to adjust settings based on their child's reactions and preferences. This adaptability not only helps in managing sensory overload but also encourages a sense of control and agency in children, empowering them to express their needs effectively.

Social skills development is another area where apps and software have made significant strides. Through interactive games and role-playing scenarios, children can practice essential social interactions in a low-pressure setting. These tools provide immediate feedback, allowing children to learn from their experiences and improve their communication abilities over time. As they engage with peers in virtual environments, they gain confidence and the skills necessary to navigate social situations in real life. For parents, this means witnessing their child develop vital skills that will serve them well into adulthood.

As you explore the vast landscape of apps and software available for learning, it's crucial to remain actively involved in your child's journey. Engage with them as they use these tools, discussing their experiences and feelings about the content.

This collaborative approach not only strengthens your bond but also provides insights into their preferences and learning styles. By embracing the potential of technology, parents can foster an enriching educational experience that supports their child's growth and development, ultimately leading them towards a brighter, more independent future.

The Future Of Technology In Autism Support

The future of technology in autism support is a realm filled with promise and potential, offering innovative solutions that can profoundly enhance the lives of individuals on the spectrum. As parents and guardians, understanding how these advancements can integrate into daily routines is vital. From communication aids to sensory-friendly environments, technology is paving the way for a more inclusive world. With every new development, we are reminded that the right tools can empower our children to express themselves, connect with others, and navigate their challenges more effectively.

One of the most significant innovations in this field is the rise of assistive communication devices and applications. These tools are designed to cater to varied communication needs, providing individuals with autism a voice. Whether through text-to-speech software or picture exchange communication systems, these technologies are revolutionizing how children interact with their families, peers, and educators. As parents, embracing these resources not only facilitates better communication but also fosters a sense of independence and confidence in our children.

Moreover, the integration of virtual reality (VR) and augmented reality (AR) into therapeutic practices is redefining social skills training. These immersive technologies create safe, controlled environments where children can practice social interactions and learn to navigate complex social cues without the pressure of real-world consequences. By simulating various scenarios, VR and

AR can help develop empathy, understanding, and adaptability, equipping our children with the skills they need to thrive in diverse social settings.

In addition to communication and social skills development, technology is also transforming educational strategies for children on the autism spectrum. Personalized learning platforms and interactive educational tools are making it easier for educators to tailor their teaching methods to fit individual learning styles. This adaptability not only enhances engagement but also allows children to progress at their own pace, ensuring that they receive the support necessary to flourish academically. As parents, advocating for the integration of these technologies in educational settings can significantly impact our children's learning experiences.

Finally, as we look towards the future, it is essential to recognize the role of technology in fostering community and support networks for parents and caregivers. Online platforms, forums, and mobile applications are creating spaces for shared experiences, advice, and resources. These communities provide invaluable emotional support and practical strategies, reminding us that we are not alone in this journey. By harnessing the power of technology, we can create a brighter, more connected future for our children and ourselves, filled with hope, understanding, and endless possibilities.

AFTERWORD

As you reach the end of this book, I hope you feel a sense of connection, hope, and empowerment. Parenting a child on the autism spectrum is a journey like no other. It is one filled with profound challenges but also incredible joys and deeply transformative experiences. Through the pages of this guide, my aim has been to walk alongside you, offering insights, tools, and encouragement to help you navigate the unique path you share with your child.

Autistic children have a way of teaching us to see the world differently,not through the lens of what is "normal" or "expected", but through the vibrant, diverse, and endlessly fascinating perspective they offer. They remind us of the beauty in details that others might overlook, the value of authenticity in a world that often prizes conformity, and the unshakable power of unconditional love.

Every step you've taken, whether it was celebrating a milestone, advocating for your child's needs, or simply holding space for their emotions, has been an act of extraordinary dedication. The moments of connection, however small or fleeting, are treasures that will shape both you and your child for years to come. This journey is not about achieving perfection; it is about progress, growth, and mutual understanding.

The spectrum is vast and varied, just as the human experience is diverse and beautiful. Your child's uniqueness is their strength, and your unwavering love is their greatest foundation. Together, you are building a life that honors who they are while empowering them to thrive in a world that may not always understand them. Know that this work you are doing, the listening, the learning, the advocating, matters deeply. It creates ripples of understanding that extend far beyond your family and into the broader world.

This book was not meant to have all the answers, because every child and every family is unique. Instead, it was meant to offer a starting point, a source of guidance and reassurance as you chart your own course. The most important lesson I hope you take away is this: you are not alone. There is a vast community of parents, advocates, educators, and allies who share your journey, and together, we can create a world that celebrates and supports autistic individuals in all their brilliance.

As you close this book, take a moment to honor yourself, for your courage, your love, and your commitment to your child's well-being. And take a moment to honor your child, who is navigating their own path with resilience, authenticity, and grace.

The journey ahead will continue to unfold in ways you cannot yet imagine, bringing with it new challenges and new triumphs. But through it all, remember this: your child is not defined by a diagnosis, nor by the perceptions of others. They are defined by their incredible spirit, their boundless potential, and the love you share with them.

Thank you for allowing me to be a part of your journey. May this book serve as a beacon of hope and a reminder of the extraordinary gift it is to love and be loved by a child on the spectrum.